DOMINION

Samson Ajetomobi

Awakening Publishing House

ISBN: 9798599241256

Cover design by: Kayode Awodeji

www.menofissacharvision.com

This book is dedicated to the Almighty God whose dominion is limitless, and to all believers who demonstrate and teach dominion in their various territories.

CONTENTS

CHAPTER ONE

THE DOMINION MANDATE

And God said, Let us make man in our image, after our likeness: and let them have dominion over the fish of the sea, and over the fowl of the air, and over the cattle, and overall the earth, and over every creeping thing that creepeth upon the earth. So God created man in his image, in the image of God created he him; male and female created he them. And God blessed them, and God said unto them, Be fruitful, and multiply, and replenish the earth, and subdue it: and have dominion over the fish of the sea, and over the fowl of the air, and over every living thing that moveth upon the earth.

GENESIS 1:26-28

God's original purpose for creating man was dominion. Thus, when He created the first man, He gave him the mandate to dominate the whole earth; God told him to be in charge of all His creations on earth; that charge was accompanied with blessings that Adam will be fruitful, he will multiply, he will replenish the earth, he will subdue it, and he will have dominion. However, Adam lost that dominion to the devil.

Dominion describes a situation of uncontested rule, absolute control and authority. This implies that dominion relates with declaring authority that cannot be resisted. The scope of dominion legalizes a man to walkover organized oppression and every established resistance. In the context of ancient warfare, a man that has dominion is a conqueror and enjoys the bounties and spoils of war.

Dominion is one of the prominent natures of God. Thus, when He made man, He made him in His likeness to have ruler-ship and to exercise dominion like Himself on earth. God lives in the heaven of heavens with the whole earth as his footstool and rules in the affairs of the entire world. This shows that dominion is not a strange vocabulary in the kingdom. If you belong to the kingdom, you should live in dominion.

In the beginning of creation, God said to man,
... Be fruitful, and multiply, and replenish the earth, and subdue it: and have dominion over the fish of the sea, and over the fowl of the air, and over every living thing that moveth upon the earth.

GENESIS 1:28

The creatures that God mentioned are figurative descriptions of the spheres God wants man to dominate. God wants man to have dominion over anything that is in the atmosphere, including spiritual forces that are in the heavenly; treasures in the sea such as oil, gold and every other thing that the sea holds; and things that move physically, anything that this physical earth can hold. God created man to have dominion; that is God's mandate for man. It was not a counsel, or a suggestion; it is a mandate. Hence, if you do less than that, you live lesser than your original calling.

Fruitfulness Leads to Dominion

And God blessed them, and God said unto them, Be fruitful, and multiply, and replenish the earth, and subdue it: and have dominion over the fish of the sea, and over the fowl of the air, and over every living thing that moveth upon the earth.

GENESIS 1:28

The features of a blessed life are fruitfulness, multiplication, subdual and dominion. The first proof that you are blessed is fruitfulness. Therefore, any life that is not fruitful disappoints the purpose of the blessing. Fruitfulness leads to multiplication which places you at a vantage position to subdue your territory, establishing your dominion in that territory.

There is a myopic understanding of what God meant when He said man should be fruitful. Contrary to what many interpret it to mean, fruitfulness in this context does not mean bearing children only. At least Jesus did not have a wife, nor did He give birth to any physical child, yet He was a fruitful man.

Fruitfulness is a culture in God's kingdom.

Fruitfulness is not a suggestion or advice; fruitfulness is a command in God's kingdom. This was why Jesus cursed a fig tree (Mark 11:12-25). Jesus had seen the tree from afar and desired to get fruit from it, but when He walked towards it, there was no fruit on the tree. Jesus frowned at the tree's fruitlessness; therefore, He cursed the tree that thenceforth nobody would eat from it again, it will not serve its generation because it refused to deliver fruit." That is how God views fruitlessness.

Fruitfulness begins with the mind. A fruitful mind does not need violence to dominate; he needs creativity and revealed ideas that can make every other thing submit. Fruitfulness is progressive and does not just happen overnight. The starting point of fruit-bearing is seed sowing. There is no fruit without a seed. Any fruit you see is the product of seed. Do not be deceived, whatsoever a man sows, he will reap. If he sows wrongly, he will reap wrongly. No form of explanation can reverse this. The seed you sow determines the kind of fruit that you see around you.

Fruits are Functions of Seeds

Seeds are important elements in the production of fruits. In the natural, no farmer goes to the farm without seeds in his hands, if he expects harvest in a later time. This is also applicable to every other area of life. In other sectors outside agriculture, fruits are results or outcomes of investments (seed). Thus, there are diverse seeds you can sow aside from what you plant in your garden.

The Seed of Character

Every time most people hear seed, they think of money first. Money is the least seed to sow. Stop measuring your Christianity with how much you have, as money fails. Church leaders should not allow any influential person dictate the tune in the church because of their money. The church belongs to Jesus. If such rich bags not give their money to the church, the church will still survive. When people go to church, it should be with a mind to learn and be better Christian, and not to oppress others. Good Character is golden; it is to be treasured above rubies.

Women who are beautiful outwardly but lack good character are liable to destroy their own home. Such women become bossy in their homes. They fight for control with their husbands at home.

Good character is everything. You are blessed when you can control your emotions, your temper and your anger.

Sow good character in church. Do not join other people to talk arrogantly about your pastor or join others to rebel against him. Demonstrate good character to the less privileged in church; do not intimidate and oppress them. Embrace them and strengthen their hearts. Empower them if you can, but do not ridicule them.

The Seed of Time

Time is a constant factor on earth, and as all sane human knows, it does not wait for anyone. Whether you decide to sleep, walk, sit before your television, or do many other things, time will not stop just a millisecond for you; it keeps counting. When time is done counting, you wake up and you realize that you are older than you were yesterday. Some spend their time in the clubhouse, drinking and laughing away their future. It only explains how smart or dull they are because smart people choose where they go; dull people stay anywhere they can laugh to while away the hours. For such people, life is funfair but in truth, life is not for fun. Wisely sow the seed of time, because whatsoever you use your time for, will return to you.

The Seed of Diligence

This world will not honour a lazy man. Even if he gets money by any illegitimate means, he will be grounded with time. Certain types of increase will not last long. Some men rose to stardom and became wealthy suddenly but are begging for survival today because the root of their wealth was not correct. Be slow to make quick money, because money itself is a spirit.

Sow the seed of diligence, as nobody honours a man who hangs around begging for money. Some, at the age of 45 are still saying, "Uncle your boy is here." Can you imagine a 45 years old man still calling himself a boy? Manliness is not a function of age; it is the function of the strength of your heart and your delivery capacity. Your delivery capacity cannot be efficient if you are not diligent. It is only the diligent that stands before great people. If a man is diligent, he will stand before great people. If a young man is diligent, he will also be brought before great people.

Some ladies are assumed to be very dutiful at work as they are seen climbing the ladder fast. They never told their husbands that the secret of their "miraculously" fast and consistent promotions is sleeping with their managers. Such people are disappointments to their generation. Any opportunity or position you are not qualified for but given to you through the wrong process will keep you disadvantaged with time. Diligent people do not cut corners because, in the end, they might have to travel more distance than they ought to go through initially.

The Seed Dies to Have Dominion
Seeds are created to die after they are sowed into the earth (John 12:44). If they do not die, nothing will come from that seed. Thus, fruitfulness requires the death of seeds.

To have kingdom dominion, you must die to yourself. In the natural, dead people lose the power of choice – they do not choose what happens to them after they die. They might have given instructions to the people around them before they died, but once they cease to breathe, they lose that ability to choose anything. Only dead men can express dominion on earth the way God wants it. God cannot trust a man who is still arrogant and strong in himself with dominion because he will be corrupted and eventually misrepresent the kingdom.

You must die to self to have true dominion. You are intelligent but you do not have to lean on your intelligence. Dominion is not first intelligence-based; it is God-based. Dominion is God's essence. Thus, if God is spiritual, then His essence is also spiritual. Dominion is spiritual. You cannot access dominion that comes from God carnally. Die to self! With your intelligence, you are still limited in knowledge because man was created with limitations – he is not all-knowing. This should inform man's choice to depend on the All-Knowing God.

CHAPTER TWO

INDICES OF LOSS OF DOMINION

It is a myth to conclude that just a few were born to rule. That was not God's original design. The command to have dominion and be in charge is for all men. Although it might be in a different capacity, but man was designed to have dominion. This includes every member of your family.

You must intentionally acknowledge that dominion fits your family too. Everyone born out of your loins can have dominion. Your family should not be a place where everybody is a struggler. If that has been the case in your family, it can come to an end by the revelation of the word of God and fervent effectual prayers.

You should not have a situation where just one of your children is doing well, while the others are struggling. No! God did not intend that your family will produce just one successful person – a local champion amid many strugglers. Father Abraham's lineage demonstrated to us that everyone from your loins can walk in degrees of dominion in different capacity.

Your family may have once lost dominion because of the disobedience or error of someone who stood in the place of headship in your family, but that dominion can also be restored.

The First Man Lost It

Dominion is tied to instructions. The moment one begins to deviate from the instructions that brought one into dominion, a fall is inevitable. Thus, to remain in dominion, we must remain within the ambit of the instructions that are tied to our dominion. Disobedience to instruction robs a man of dominion.

Adam, the first man and father, lost the dominion God bequeathed on him to the devil because he disobeyed instruction (check Genesis chapter three). Disobedience is like breaking a hedge because dominion is a hedge.

Adam did not understand the gravity and consequences of the thing he did; so instead of soberly admitting his mistake to God, he started playing the blame game. Adam indirectly blamed God for giving him a woman in the first place, and he directly blamed his wife, Eve. He did all that to exonerate himself. This just compounded the error of the first man. Since the head of the family has chosen to justify himself, Eve was not ready to take the whole blame to herself; so she joined in playing the game too.

As long as you keep shifting blames to the next person as reason for losing dominion, God's attention will keep shifting from you to the next person. The power to regain what you lost lies with God. The more you shift His attention from you to people or things that you claim made you lost your dominion, the farther you send His help away from you.

Heads of families must rise to the occasion – once you realize that your family has no shade of dominion left, take responsibility for it. Leave the dead who traded the dominion of your family on the altar of an ancient idol to lie still in their grave. The responsibility to determine the destiny of your family now falls on you; do not waste time playing the blame game, else your children and generations after you will not speak well of you. Stand before God and admit to Him that you were in the loins of your forefathers when they were committing those grievous errors on the altar of blood sacrifices. Take responsibility and cry to God for mercy.

One of the servants of Elisha was wise to take responsibility when the axe head fell into the water. He cried out, "Alas it was borrowed", and his master, Elisha, asked him where the axe head had fallen. He did not say it was when somebody else took it from me; he said, “Here” (2 Kings 6:1-7). Once you know the root of the problem confronting you, the cure is close by.

There are consequences for disobedience of instruction. When Adam broke the hedge of dominion around his life, he began to experience unusual things around him.

Nakedness

The first thing Adam realized after he lost dominion was that he was naked. When you lose dominion, you will be exposed. Not only you; your family will be exposed too. You and your family become vulnerable to attacks. Things that should not mess you up will mess you up.

Adam led Eve to go and hide because they were ashamed and afraid. That is what happens to a family that has lost dominion. No sane man walks confidently on the street without clothing. But in the spiritual realm, there are lots of families walking naked because they have broken the hedge of dominion that provides cover for them.

The result of this in the natural is that such family will be without honour and respect in the society. People will treat them anyhow, talk to them as common men, shut them down whenever they want to say anything and they will be considered insignificant in the society because they have lost their coverage in the spiritual realm – their dominion has been taken away.

Insecurity

Another grievous consequence of Adam's disobedience was that he lost his domain. Dominion is expressed in a domain. Once you go out of that domain, you lose your influence and authority. Eden was Adam's domain of dominion. The moment he stepped out of that domain, he became a mere man. In that domain of dominion he was shielded. He was kept. He was protected. He enjoyed God's presence as his covering and shield in Eden. It was like a fortress. Outside Eden, Adam needed to learn to survive; he needed to devise ways to protect himself and his family – that was an extra burden for him. No human security, no matter how sophisticated it is can substitute for God's presence that keeps a man. The watchmen will keep watch in futility except the Lord keeps the city (Psalms 127:1-2).

Toiling

When a man loses dominion he begins to labour with physical strength and energy for things he should have gotten by grace. Then, when Adam lost dominion, the Lord told him he will labouriously till the ground before the ground would supply what he needed for survival (Genesis 3:17-19).

A man that loses dominion works hard just to get a little supply. This is a very critical lesson to learn from Adam.

Disorderliness in Family

Disorderliness at home is one of the signs that dominion has been lost. Adam had a small nuclear family of just two sons, but those boys never agreed. Adam had just Cain and Abel, but they witch-hunted each other until Cain killed Abel (Genesis 4:1-8). That is the kind of dissension and disorderliness you see in the family of a man that has lost dominion. His children will not value one another nor will they relate like good friends. Though born into the same family and by same parent, they will find it difficult to say relate with one another. They will not help each other but fight against each other. They suspect one another and deviously seek ways to run down themselves, simply because they cannot just stand the rise of their siblings.

This was the same thing that happened in the house of Isaac. He had only two sons, Esau and Jacob, but they were two parallel lines that started their dispute from the womb. As common as a plate of pottage was, Jacob used it to trick his brother into trading his birthright (Genesis 25:2o-34). What cruelty!

When people lose dominion there will be no commitment to improve each other, not even their twin siblings. Rather, they have a singular commitment – endless contentions to ensure that the other siblings do not rise above them.

Loss of dominion has a greater impact on a family. Instead of peace at home, they will experience chaotic disputes even on food matters and other petty issues.

Grievous Debt

Now there cried a certain woman of the wives of the sons of the prophets unto Elisha, saying, Thy servant my husband is dead; and thou knowest that thy servant did fear the Lord: and the creditor is come to take unto him my two sons to be bondmen. And Elisha said unto her, What shall I do for thee? tell me, what hast thou in the house? And she said, Thine handmaid hath not anything in the house, save a pot of oil. Then he said, Go, borrow thee vessels abroad of all thy neighbours, even empty vessels; borrow not a few. And when thou art come in, thou shalt shut the door upon thee and upon thy sons, and shalt pour out into all those vessels, and thou shalt set aside that which is full. So she went from him, and shut the door upon her and upon her sons, who brought the vessels to her; and she poured out.

2 KINGS 4:1-5

Here is an interesting story of a great man of God – a prophet who prophesied to people and it came to pass, yet he died in poverty. If you go into ministry just because you are looking for a cheap way to make money, you will still end up being poor.

This man did all the prophesying and the prophecies came to pass but when he died, his wife visited Elisha crying of a loss and debt. She told Elisha that he too can testify that her husband feared the Lord. This implies that you can fear God and still die poor. Hence, it is not enough to just fear God; there are other things you must do for God to bring you into financial dominion.

...You all know a good man he was...

2 KINGS 4:1 (MSG)

Being a good man is not a proof that you have dominion. Can you imagine the testimony of this man – he was a good man, he took care of all the people, but he did not take care of his own family. He prophesied to other people, but the anointing did not benefit his wife and children and his home. Here is a sacred counsel for you – take care of your vineyard, because you are getting old, and the earlier you take care the better it is for you.

That late prophet was a good man, devoted to God, but while he was doing all that, he was borrowing money here and there. However, contrary to the concept of borrowing, I believe that every believer should resolve to have this mindset that anything God cannot supply, do not go around looking for it by any means. Do not go into debt because you will become a slave to the lender.

Mortgaged Future

...is on his way to collect my two son's...

2 KINGS 4:1 (MSG)

A price was placed on the children of the late prophet, not because they committed treason, but because they had a father, who though anointed, lacked the right skills to judiciously manage and invest resources. Any money that comes to his house goes into the purchase of a new suit, a new shoe; he appeared like a big boy, but he was very small within. Every time, he just wants to change his car to harass people.

Most times, many people over-magnify themselves before other people, thereby hurting themselves, because they would want to do all they can to sustain the false character of themselves they presented to people. Those people who they are trying to impress would always place demand on them based on the character shown them. Thus, you only end up thinning out.

Be contented with whichever car God blesses you with; use it with gratefulness. Do not buy a car because your neighbour bought a new one; you are not headed the same direction. Wives, stop mounting pressure on your husband by comparing them with your neighbours. It is natural for sensible husbands to try to impress their wives by doing anything to make them happy, but if their wives keep mounting pressure on them, they will be forced to do things they might not be able to handle later.

Do not borrow a cloth to impress anybody. Young ladies, if a guy goes to borrow a coat and tie just to propose to you, tell him to come back the following day. By then the owner of the coat would have collected it, and you will see his normal regular clothes.

When a man loses dominion, his future is mortgaged. Your children are your future, do not mortgage them. When your children are taken away from you, it marks the beginning of the end of your life, because there will be no one left to carry on your legacies. For the wife of that prophet to lose her husband was enough pain for her to deal with, but for her sons, who ought to be her consolation, to be taken away from her, and be used for a down payment for the bill her late husband could not pay, is a more grievous pain that could have claimed her life.

Our parents sinned and are no more, and now we're paying for the wrongs they did.

LAMENTATIONS 5:4-6

Today, some children are suffering what their parents caused, while their parents have passed away.

Every child reading this book should earnestly pray not to inherit the debts of their parents; that God will help their parents out of every kind of debt before they depart this world.

CHAPTER THREE

RESTORING DOMINION

And the angel of the Lord appeared unto him, and said unto him, The Lord is with thee, thou mighty man of valour.

JUDGES 6:12

The first point of call in restoring dominion is to know who you are. Your current situation can sometimes mask your real identity, thereby making you define your life by what you are going through. However, God sees you differently. Thus, to come into dominion, God must reveal to you who you are.

You are not what your problem and environment says you are. You are the redeemed of the Lord. You were purchased with the blood of Jesus (1 Corinthians 6:20; Hebrews 9:12) and you have been made unto God a royal entity of glory (1 Peter 2:9).

And Gideon said unto him, Oh my Lord, if the Lord be with us, why then is all this befallen us? and where be all his miracles which our fathers told us of, saying, Did not the Lord bring us up from Egypt? but now the Lord hath forsaken us, and delivered us into the hands of the Midianites.

JUDGES 6:13

Also, one of the traits of those who rebel against yokes that bar them and their family from walking in kingdom dominion is inquisitiveness. That was the attitude of Gideon when an angel came to him with the message of deliverance.

Gideon even went further to ask about the great miracles their fathers told them God did among them, and the great wonders God wrought in Egypt. He wondered what had gone wrong that none of those testimonies are evident in his days. Just like Gideon, those are the same kind of questions people are asking the church. People want the men of God to bring an assuring and definite message from God that can turn things around in the nations of the world.

God's response to Gideon was, "Go in this thy might..." (Judges 6:14). It is the person that is disturbed about a situation that God will give the key to proffer solution to the situation.

Anyone that does not have dominion mentality will think and talk the way Gideon did in the Bible text above. Who told you divine nomination has to do with the financial state of your family? God's nomination has nothing to do with your present financial state; that is why you have to be careful not to monetize everything that God is doing in your life. Your position in your family does not matter in God's nomination of who He will use to orchestrate deliverance. Thus, do not even think you are disadvantaged.

The focus here is what must be done to come into dominion. God disregarded the grumblings and excuses of Gideon and told him that the main issue is that there is an altar in his father's house that sustains poverty, and God told him to pull it down.

Stop lamenting about your poverty; in truth, poverty has a spiritual dimension. Some people are so hardworking and full of energy, yet they are still poor. Like Gideon, you will have to bring down that altar first, before you can walk in dominion.

Esau's Discovery

And by thy sword shalt thou live, and shalt serve thy brother; and it shall come to pass when thou shalt have the dominion, that thou shalt break his yoke from off thy neck.

GENESIS 27:40

This is the story of a man whose blessing was stolen by his brother. His father had told him to bring him venison. He asked him to go hunt for something, kill it, prepare it and let him eat out of his labour (Genesis 27:3).

Honouring your parents who nurtured you with the fruits of your labour is a critical step in entering dominion (Ephesians 6:1). They gave birth to you; they could have decided to abort you, but they kept you instead and allowed you to live. This is enough reason to take care of them.

Esau worked so hard to bring his father the venison, only to be told his brother had cunningly stolen his blessing. Do not forget the features of a blessed life: fruitfulness, multiplication, subdual and dominion. Esau's brother received all those elements before he returned. When he eventually returned, Isaac, his father, told him he had blessed his brother, Jacob, and it cannot be reversed. His father bluntly told him that he would serve his brother and his brother would be greater than him, and before he could experience just a little breakthrough, he would need to work hard. What an anomaly!

Have you seen people like that? For them to experience just a little breakthrough, they will have to work hard. Then you see some other people who do not work as hard as they do enjoy so much blessing. The first group will begin to wonder, "But Lord, what happened to me? Why is everything hard when it comes to my turn?" Do you find yourself in this same category? You might have laboured academically, but it is just hard to succeed. You might have tried your hands on a business venture, but it is hard. You might have laboured in ministry or just about anything you touch seems so hard. Yours is not the first case; Esau also went through the same thing. This should make you stay glued to this book to find out if Esau eventually broke that yoke of servitude and endless struggles.

Isaac frankly told Esau, "Son, the blessing was meant for you, but your brother played me; he got the blessing and there is nothing we can do. But here is my counsel for you, you will be living by the sword to survive; life may be hard and tough for you, but the day an understanding comes to you and you fight back to break the yoke that has kept you in servitude and restricted you, you will enter into dominion."

Do you have the understanding yet to fight the yoke of hardship? Are you saying, "Lord this is not my best, I can be greater than I am now; I need to break that yoke"? Isaac described what would slow down Esau's journey in life and make him toil endlessly as a yoke. This portrays yokes as something burdensome. The yoke life and some family challenges place on many people is not something pleasurable; it is burdensome. It slows them down and makes them struggle.

Yokes are designed to restrict movements. The yokes from this world and its prince can never be easy and light, only Jesus offers a yoke that is light and easy. Anything you are yoked to that is not of God will limit your life journey. Those yokes can be broken today, in the name of Jesus.

That was all Isaac told Esau; THE YOKE CAN BE BROKEN. Whatever you are yoked to restricting your journey in life can be broken. IT CAN BE BROKEN! Once he heard that the yoke can be broken, he set out to kill the person who stole his blessing; perhaps the blessing will be reversed. However, that was not the solution.

Killing men does not solve the problem because what they took from you is not physical but spiritual. The spiritual rules the natural; so trying to revenge against your brother or against somebody else that did something bad against you is not a smart decision. You can dismantle anyone who stole from you by spiritual principle without any physical fight or any words from your mouth. Go spiritual!

Esau Obtained Dominion

And the messengers returned to Jacob, saying, We came to thy brother Esau, and also he cometh to meet thee, and four hundred men with him.

GENESIS 32:6

Esau was going to meet Jacob after twenty years of separation and he took with him four hundred military-like men as his entourage. Jacob had sent an advance party to do a survey and was told his brother was coming to meet him with four hundred armed men. Jacob thought nemesis had caught up with him and decided to deploy a trick. He kept one of the servant ladies he married with her children, the other servant lady with her children, Leah with her children, and then he kept Rachael last. The calculation was that by the time Esau and his four hundred men was killing the first group, he would have been running. When they advance to kill the next band, he would have gone far and by the time they finished killing all his family, he would have gone out of sight.

You do not know who loves you until the water gets bad. Jacob would have professed his love for them and even flattered them that he could die for them since it cost him many years of labour to marry his wives. Little wonder some women do not trust men. Do not blame them! Rather, ask them about their experiences with men, before you arrive at any conclusion.

Esau's greatness had made Jacob forget his love for his family. A poor man cannot keep four hundred men in his house. There is the possibility that those four hundred armed men with Esau have wives. If they have one wife each, that will be at least eight hundred people. Assuming each of them has two children, that is a big household. You can imagine what it will cost you to have a company where you pay one thousand six hundred members of staff every month. For Esau, he was not paying them monthly; they eat in his house every day.

The day Esau met with Jacob, he made a profound statement, "I have enough..." (Genesis 33:9).

Esau's entourage revealed his financial capacity and his depth of network. The yoke that once limited his dominion must have been broken. Esau's transformation is a proof that limiting yokes can be broken and lost dominion can be recovered. You too can enter the dimension of dominion. **Just Break It!**

No special ritual or ceremony is required to break the yoke that has held you bound for many years. Just break it. Esau got angry at his situation and he started a journey to break the yoke. You do not need to join any occult group or club; just break the yoke! You do not have to keep suspecting any of your relatives or your neighbours; just break the yoke.

Being lethargic about the situation in your life shows you are still contented with the situation and satisfied with the "we are managing" slang. However, if Esau's story provokes your inner man, then it is time for you to rebel against that yoke to see the end of its influence over your life and destiny.

And Jabez was more honourable than his brethren: and his mother called his name Jabez, saying, Because I bare him with sorrow. And Jabez called on the God of Israel, saying, Oh that thou wouldest bless me indeed, and enlarge my coast, and that thine hand might be with me, and that thou wouldest keep me from evil, that it may not grieve me! And God granted him that which he requested.

1 CHRONICLES 4:9-10

Jabez's story was only described in two verses of the Chronicles, but those two verses reveals the full scope of all that we need to do to break yokes. Jabez's yoke was enshrined in and specially customized with his name by his mother. His mother placed a grievous yoke of bitterness, gross pain and severe afflictions on him. You see here the power of the words of parents have over their seeds. What has this innocent child done to incur such burdensome yoke other than to just have been born in the natural way every other woman gives birth to their children too?

Of importance in this story is how Jabez got angry about his situation and called on the God of Israel to break the yoke. He started his prayer with an exclamation to indicate the grievousness of the yoke. Jabez did not just pray casually; he prayed earnestly. He had great burden upon his soul – burdens that were so wearisome. He had just four prayer points and God granted him all his requests. Jabez prayed! To break that yoke, you too must pray earnestly. Do not be contented with your present situation if you know you struggle to put food on your table not to talk of feeding members of your family. If you know you try to hide your face when your siblings and extended family members are talking about contributing a sum to organize a special function, do not keep quiet. If you know that you are struggling in any area of your life, you should rise to pray earnestly! Just break it!

Rebel against those yokes, and break them to begin to live out the blessings of God on your life.

Henceforth, you will not beg men for bread to survival! The yoke that held you down, that sustains poverty around your life, shall be broken. The yoke that made your life journey very hard and tough is broken today! The yoke that is threatening your marriage and making your children to become vagabonds everywhere is broken today, in the name of Jesus.

CHAPTER FOUR

THE MARKS OF DOMINION

Saying with a loud voice, Worthy is the Lamb that was slain to receive power, and riches, and wisdom, and strength, and honour, and glory, and blessing.

REVELATION 5:12

Christ's death and resurrection guarantees some privileges to anyone who receives him. The worth of his death and resurrection bequeathed seven unique things – power, riches, wisdom, strength, honour, glory and blessing to us as mark of our dominion. To access all, you must have a relationship with Jesus. Since Jesus procured all those marks for us through his death and resurrection, you have to believe Jesus died and resurrected to restore dominion to man.

With this, no power of hell, no scheme of men, no level of manipulation of men, can pluck you out of His hand.

Power

Christianity can be very frustrating without the

power of God. Jesus was slain to give us power to reign on earth, but the phrase that precedes power in the aforementioned scripture is *to receive*.

When someone says he or she wants to give you something, it is within your power to either receive it or reject it. Power is essential for dominion and Jesus has offered it to you; receive it. Jesus said that you will receive power after the Holy Spirit comes upon you (Acts 1:8). The Holy Spirit is the custodian of the power Jesus offered. He embodies all that Jesus procured for man. Go for power!

Riches

To live in dominion is to have access to wealth. The lamb that was slain gave you access to true riches. It is your right to have riches. It is not humility not to be rich, as Christianity is not tantamount to poverty. Godliness does not mean being gullible. If you are not enjoying wealth as you ought to, you need to seek to know the reason. Jesus became poor so that you can be made rich (2 Corinthians 8:9). If you are not enjoying the riches, you are making Jesus' work to be wasted in your life.

Wisdom

No matter your skill, resources, or wealth, if you are foolish in decision making, you will destroy all that God planted around you. You need wisdom to live your life and manage every form of increase you experience. You need wisdom to accurately dispense

God's power in your life.

Marriages fail for lack of wisdom. A large percentage of failed marriages are not demonic attacks, but lack of wisdom. When you lack wisdom, you will take your spouse and children for granted. Wise fathers do not threaten a matured child. If a man lacks wisdom, he will marry a second wife to celebrate his wealth.

When riches increase, a foolish man will go and buy a fleet of cars to make a statement. You do not know some strange things you are capable of doing until you have access to some resources. Wealth has a spirit; people can imagine doing some strange things because riches came into their hands.

Therefore, to have lasting dominion, wisdom is inevitable. Only a wise man is normal under supernatural supplies; a foolish soul loses all supplies because he or she is loose.

Strength

You can be wealthy, you can have power, you can have wisdom, but when you are deficient of physical strength you will still be grossly restricted.

Strength is very important to walk in dominion. It is because of strength you can move around. Strength enables your mobility from one point to another via are walking, jogging or running. It also makes it possible for you to enjoy your riches and to display wisdom.

The strength mentioned here is not limited to just physical strength but includes spiritual strength. Paul prayed for members of the Ephesians church be strengthened in their inner man (Ephesians 3:16). There is a strengthening from the inside that goes beyond your physical strength.

When the enemy shows up against you, it is the inner strength that will help you dare the enemy. You will need inner strength in different seasons of your life, especially when the enemy comes like a roaring lion threatening to take away all that you hold dear. It is during such days you need to demonstrate much strength. When you fail in such days, your strength is little (Proverbs 24:10).

All the strength you need to walk in dominion has been made available in Jesus; take advantage of this provision.

Honour

Honour is good and it is a sign of dominion. Honour comes from God and is the panacea for reproach and shame. The finished work of Jesus Christ on the cross enlists you for honour. He made you a king and a priest unto God (Revelation 1:6). What a position of honour. If a man finds honour and he knows not, he will die like a beast (Psalms 49:20). Honour looks good on man; it looks good on you.

Do not let people rubbish you because you are royalty. Put some dignity on yourself. Put on honour as a garment. This is different from being proud. The proud has no place with God because He resists the proud. Nevertheless, live honourably; live a life that cannot be ridiculed.

Let honour flow in your home. Do things that will make your wife and children honour you. Do not do any ignoble thing that can make you lose honour at the home front and in the society. Your spouse and children will not honour you when you keep creating a tumultuous atmosphere in your home. To live honourably at home is to understand the role of your spouse in your life. In truth, nobody can help you like your spouse who will stay longer with you when everyone else leaves. As a man, it is more honourable to treat your wife as a queen. Women are deep thinkers and wise; you are a blessed man even to your fourth-generation if your wife is full of wisdom.

Women are great helpers. If you want to make a great decision, carry your wife along; she will give you a bigger picture that will surprise you and help you. Do not ever try to ask your wife to "shut up!" Wise and honourable men value the counsels of their wives.

When a misunderstanding ensued between Abraham and Sarah over Hagar and Ishmael, God sent an angel from heaven to the house of Abraham just to make one statement, and then return to heaven. The statement was, "Listen to Sarah thy wife" (Genesis 21:12). Listening to your wife will make you more honourable before her. You cannot demand this honour, you have to earn it.

This is same in every other place you walk into. Do not demand honour, live honourable and people will honour you.

Glory

There is the glory of the sun, there is the glory of the moon, there is the glory of the star, and one star differs from another (1 Corinthians 15:41). Glory is illuminations that can alter your outlook and make you emerge with greater value than you were. Your colleagues who used to know you will see you and address you differently – with dignity and honour, because of the glory.

There are dimensions of glory. There is the celestial glory and there is the terrestrial glory. There is nothing wrong with earthly glory; you can enjoy it too. Do not write yourself off. Do not say it is too late for you to experience glory. No! It does not matter how old you are, you can still enjoy glory and honour.

Blessing

Blessing is more than a salutation, blessing is a force. When blessing comes upon your life, you cannot be cursed. God's blessing on a man makes him positively different.

There is the story of a powerful prophet known as Balaam, who was hired by a king called Balak to curse the people of God for him. When the prophet closed his eyes to curse God's people, the Lord came to him and told him that he cannot curse the people He has blessed. (Numbers 23 and 22)

When Jacob began to wrestle with the angel of God and was demanding that the angel must bless him, he knew the significance of what he was asking (Genesis 32:22-30). Right from the day Jacob was blessed, he stopped being Jacob; he became a prince with God. He attained a spiritual stature that could only be traced to God, which nobody could mess up.

CHAPTER FIVE

DREAM DOMINION

It is worthy of note to emphatically state here that nobody comes into dominion without a dream. Men who do not have any dream do not go far. Dreams here refer refers to what you see your life becoming in years to come; the images of how you will emerge to become greater than who you are now.

And Joseph dreamed a dream, and he told it his brethren: and they hated him yet the more. And he said unto them, Hear, I pray you, this dream which I have dreamed: For, behold, we were binding sheaves in the field, and, lo, my sheaf arose, and also stood upright; and, behold, your sheaves stood round about, and made obeisance to my sheaf. And his brethren said to him, Shalt thou indeed reign over us? or shalt thou indeed have dominion over us? And they hated him yet the more for his dreams, and for his words. And he dreamed yet another dream, and told it his brethren, and said, Behold, I have dreamed a dream more; and, behold, the sun and the moon and the eleven stars made obeisance to me.

GENESIS 37:5-8

As a child of God, there is a time God will paint pictures of your future upon the canvass of your mind. This picture becomes something you begin to dream of and aspire to become. Without these pictures upon the canvass of your mind, you will not aspire for anything great in life. You must envision who you want to be; otherwise, you will remain miles away from dominion without a dream.

Everyone who exercised dominion in the bible had dreams; they had visions that set their lives on course; they received a word of prophecy that guided them into the life of dominion.

From the story of Joseph, we understood that dreams are precious, thus they cannot be treated carelessly.

Guard your Dreams with Discretion

Joseph had a dream but he was not matured enough to handle what he had seen. He enthusiastically told other members of his family, who were older than him. The dream infuriated his brothers; his enthusiasm was misinterpreted as arrogance, thus, they hated him for his dreams and mannerism.

Their primary concern was how their little brother could ever conceive having dominion over them. That is preposterous! This is the reality found in the human society today too. Some people will kill for an opportunity to just snuff out your life simply because they envy your dreams. They feel threatened at what you will become.

The wise men that went to make inquiry at the palace of King Herod about the kingly star of a child they had seen in the Far East made the King turn blue – he became restless and felt extremely threatened that a potential king has arrived to usurp his throne. Rarely does anyone smile at the sight of another person who has the potential to fill the same position they currently occupy. King Herod's fear triggered his anger and jealousy for the newborn baby. He tried to subtly get the location of the child, but he failed. He became more furious and ordered the manslaughter of every child who was two years and below (Matthew 2:1-16).

Joseph was not discrete in handling his dreams. He allowed emotions to becloud his discernment. He should have kept the second dream to himself, seeing that his brothers frowned at him when he told them his first dream. The reason most people do not make much progress in life is because of their indiscretion in handling God's blessings. Like Joseph, they just run their mouths loosely to every human that has ears without knowing the thoughts in the heart of those people.

You do not need to announce God’s blessing on your life. When the blessing is fully matured, it will announce itself and all eyes will see it. By then, no one will be able to kill it because it has reached full maturity. While God is still in the process of beautifying your life, keep quiet; keep thanking God and trusting Him in anticipation of the fullness of the blessings, else you will fight unnecessary battles.

When Joseph's brothers saw him coming they did not see him as Joseph anymore; they sarcastically called him the dreamer (Genesis 37:18-20).

This statement indicates that they do not have any issue with Joseph the boy but with Joseph the dreamer. Their contention is primarily his dreams. Your dream is a threat to some people; guard it jealously.

Dreams Do not Die

Joseph's dream changed the course of his life. Although his brothers concocted different mischievous plans to abort those dreams, his dreams remained potent and alive. They threw him into a dry well, ripped him of his coat of many colours and soiled it with the blood of an animal as a deceptive charade for their malevolence before they finally sold him off. Joseph was sold into Egypt as a slave, but his dreams were not enslaved.

His narrative further worsened when he was falsely accused and sentenced to the royal prison. Yet, even in the prison, his dreams were a burning and a shining light that could not be incarcerated. Joseph's experiences were testaments to the fact that dreams do not die in the hearts of the men who dreamt it. Dreams have voices and do speak. Joseph's dreams spoke even in the prison.

His dreams made him stand to speak before the King of the nation that had one of the foremost civilizations in history – Pharaoh of Egypt. His dreams kept nudging him forward. What is pushing you forward? Do you have any dream for your life? When people around you sarcastically query you if anything could come out of your Nazareth, you should raise your head with strong faith, and respond courageously that yes, a saviour came out of it once! If that boy could come out of a home with numerous older brothers who did not like him, and he later went on to become the prime minister of a foreign country, then, anything can come out of this Nazareth too. All he had that kept him going was his dreams.

Keep your dreams alive too. That is one of your tools to entering dominion.

Pursue your Dreams

To walk in true dominion, you must go beyond dreaming. You must possess the inner courage to pursue your dreams. The courage must come from within because victory starts from the mind.

For those that had a dream but just concluded that it is impossible or doubted its fruition, their minds need to be transformed because dominion begins from the mind. If your mind can receive it, you will experience it. Anything your mind cannot receive, you cannot experience. Do not add yourself to the list of people who had great dreams but never saw it materialize.

God's Presence secures your dreams

God changed Jacob's life with just one dream (Genesis 28:10-22). The images Jacob saw in his dream that night was nothing he was familiar with in the physical realm. He saw a ladder so tall that it touched heaven and earth. He saw angels ascending and descending on that ladder and then he saw a being that looked like God standing at the top of that ladder. What a magnificent encounter! Little wonder Jacob, who was renowned for subtlety and cunningness, acknowledged after he came out of that dream, "Surely the Lord is in this place; and I knew it not."

It was through that dream Jacob got a picture of what his latter days will look like and what he had to do to realize what God told him. Most importantly, God assured him that he would be with him. That dream redefined and reshaped his whole life.

The security of your dream is in having God's presence with you. Diverse situations can arise that will overwhelm you so much that you lose sight of God's presence. Some situations could be so overwhelming that they even make you question if God exists. Do not fret; He is there with you (Isaiah 40:1-5). Inasmuch God is with you, your dream is secured and dominion is possible.

Follow Your Dreams Not the Norms

Out of Jacob shall come him that have dominion and shall destroy him that remains of the city.

NUMBERS 24:19

Of the twelve sons of Jacob, only one emerged having true dominion. A look at the occupational history of Jacob's family shows how just one in that lineage deviated to take another path. Jacob was a herdsman and his first ten sons also followed in his footsteps. Joseph stayed at home with his dad, not because he was lazy, but his path was just different from others'. His path was different because he had a dominion mindset. Eventually, it was just the one that decided to follow his dreams that ascended the throne and had great dominion.

Since the occupational heritage of his family had not made any of his predecessors ascend the throne or have great dominion, another path was carved for him.

The verbal reaction of Joseph's relatives to his dreams was an attempt to shut him up and shut down his dreams. They felt threatened and thought it was not traditional. His dreams depicted a defiance of their occupational heritage, hence the aversion to his dreams.

Jacob's blessing on Joseph was so distinct from others. Joseph, you are a fruitful vine whose tree climbs over the wall (Genesis 49:22).

By implication, when you put a barrier before a man that has dominion, if he cannot pull down the barrier he will climb over the barrier.

Joseph's ascension into dominion suggests that in every family God chooses at least one person for dominion. It was Abraham for Terah's family, Joseph for Jacob's family, and David for Jesse's family.

Your position in your family is not a core factor for determining who walks in dominion or not. Joseph was the 11th while David was the 8th in his own family, yet they were both coronated to wield degrees of dominion. Thus, the number you occupy in your family does not stop your chances of walking in dominion.

However, contrary to traditional beliefs, God does not consider someone in a family to walk in dominion to oppress or rule over other members of the family. No! If that happens, it was not God. God chooses one person in a family to bring salvation to that family, or even to an entire nation. David saved his entire family and Israel and Joseph did the same thing.

CHAPTER SIX

WALKING IN DOMINION

The essence of this book is to stress one truth – every child of God can walk in dominion. Dominion was programmed into your fabric when you became God's child. However, the devil deploys different mechanisms to make it look like a lie, so that you will neither believe it nor walk its reality.

Some years ago, a young lady demonstrated her dominion as a child of God in her Islamic family. Her father was a high-ranking Islamic cleric. He fiercely chased his daughter out of the house because she gave her life to Jesus. The young lady was undeterred by the threats of her father. She remained steadfast and continued to follow Jesus. She submitted herself for discipleship and she waxed stronger in the knowledge of God and her identity in God. With time, the young lady's younger brother passed away. Her father tried all he could to salvage the life of the boy but to no avail. The boy stayed cold dead.

At twilight, her father concluded that there was

nothing he could do again to revive the boy but to bury him. Immediately, the young lady took the opportunity to demonstrate her dominion. She asked her father to permit her to practice the things she had been learning of Jesus Christ. She courageously prayed for the boy after getting her father's permission. As the young lady asked her younger brother to wake up in the name of Jesus, the young man stood up. He came back to life and stayed alive.

This dynamic supernatural intervention made her father scream, "Praise the Lord!" He laid aside the fact that he was an Islamic cleric. He turned to his daughter to know what he should do next. That supernatural experience opened his family for salvation.

It is your right to express the life of God in you. Dominion is in your gene. Now is the time for you to walk in dominion.

Believe God's Word

Naturally, every child has the potential to do great things, but they cannot just do great things without learning. It is through learning and practice that the inherent potentials begin to find expression. This is same in the spiritual too. As children of God, we have the potentials to dominate and bring glory to God through our lives, but without knowing how, the potentials will just be dormant.

The state of your mind towards the word of God is

very crucial to walking in dominion; you must have an unwavering conviction in your mind about what God says to you, because His words to you cannot fail. Do not forget that victory begins in your mind; thus, the way you esteem God's word in your mind shows how much dominion you will command.

Do not limit God in your mind. To walk in dominion, you must believe that God can lift you out of every unbefitting position and make you to walk in dominion. Your family traditions and heritage is not too tough for God to handle. Your situation is not hopeless. Just keep believing God in every step of the way. The visions He showed you, the promises and prophecies you received from Him will surely be fulfilled, only believe.

Live in Forgiveness

Anyone that will walk in dominion, not just for a while, but for a long period must be quick to forgive. Joseph understood God lifted him from his family to walk in dominion for the salvation and preservation of lives (Genesis 45:4-5). Thus, he was quick to forgive his brothers for every evil thing they did to him.

Do not be resentful towards anyone for any evil thing they did to you while you were on your way to the throne. Bitterness is like a gall that can ruin your chances on staying long on the throne of dominion. Only men who have healthy mind can rule righteously the way God designed it. Those who find it hard to forgive those who offended them while ascending to the throne are likely to become oppressive and even do worse things than their offenders did to them.

Have an Unquenchable Prayer Life

Another secret to walking in dominion is having an unquenchable prayer life. The secret of every great man you have read about today was their secret place.

Prayer is the secret place for every believer. Jesus said when you pray, close your door, bow your knees and pray (Matthew 6:6). There is the prayer of the closet that does not need to get applause from anyone; it is a prayer where nobody sees you until your results announce you. When a man is given to prayer the result will speak.

There is a great man that kept having daily vigil for thirty years. Today, the man is a global phenomenon; you cannot push him to take the back seat anymore, as nations ask him to come address them. All these were possible because he has an unquenchable prayer life.

An unquenchable prayer life will make witches submit to you; powers of darkness will bow to you, and you will be bold as a lion to confront anything that stands in your way.

In the course of prayers, God instructs your enemies

not to do you evil. Laban had planned to kill Jacob, but the God of Jacob accosted him and instructed him not to lay a finger on Jacob (Genesis 31:24). Your prayer life makes you God's friend; and this will make God speak for you whenever someone wants to hurt you.

It is also from the place of prayer that you receive clear instructions from God on how to deal with your adversary before your adversary shows up. The Bible does not tell us what the prayer life of Shadrach, Meshach and Abednego but the degree of confidence they demonstrated before Nebuchadnezzar was nothing short of their knowledge of God and their intimacy with Him. In praying, you will gain access to visions and secrets that ordinary people do not have access to, as it happened with Daniel and his friends at Babylon.

An unquenchable prayer life secures your spouse; no one can just come and snatch them away. A powerful King tried it with God's friend, Abraham (Genesis 20:1-16). He took Abraham's wife, but God spoke on his behalf that the powerful king became jittery and reversed his actions. An unquenchable prayer life brings you into intimacy with God. You look just like the being you pray to; prayer will make you look like God. Moses prayed so much to the point that his countenance changed and radiated glory. He started to look like God because he spent a lot of days communing with God (Exodus 34:29-35). Jesus had the same experience at the Mount of Transfiguration; His physical countenance was altered – He was beaming glory (Matthew 17:1-8).

Take Prayers Seriously

Your prayer altar is very important; no one should beg you or compel you to attend prayer meetings. If you understand that prayer meeting is for your benefit, you will be more to attend. Do not ever allow the devil to dissuade you from attending prayer meetings. He can come with a lot of overwhelming thoughts to distract you and make you feel discouraged. His goal is to ensure that your prayer fire goes low; do not permit it.

Do not ever justify your prayerlessness with excuses that God understands the nature of your job and He knows that you are usually tired whenever you get back home from work. NO! God does not understand; He cannot understand a prayerless believer. Jesus had a rigorous work schedule, yet He still had the time to pray all night. So what is your excuse?

Pray with all your life and pray intelligently; do not pray without guides. Depend on the Holy Spirit to guide you through revelation and the truth He reveals to you (John 16:13), because we do not know how we ought to pray (Romans 8:26). Do not be one of those Christians who depend on other people to hear God and see visions for them. You are depriving yourself of your heritage by running to different mountains and hills and valleys just to have others hear God for you. You have access to hear God and see things about your life too. Only lazy Christians wait for people to pray for them and hear God for them. What has God said concerning your life? What has He shown you? Go into your closet and seek Him until He speaks to you.

The Syrian army once surrounded the whole mountain where Elisha was. As the servant went on an errand, he saw the Syrian army with all kinds of weapons in their hands. The servant ran inside and cried out in fear. Elisha calmly looked at the jittery young man and prayed a simple prayer for him: that he will see (2 Kings 6:15-17).

Many of us feel insecure and fearful because we are terrified by the threats of men and circumstances that threatened to consume us. If only your eyes are opened to see the mighty host of God with you, you will gallantly confront those things threatening you.

CHAPTER SEVEN

ANOINTED FOR DOMINION

For God has not given us the spirit of fear

2TIMOTHY 1:7

God is not the author of fear; it is from another source. Fear makes you to exaggerate your enemy as bigger than you. It makes you quake that your life will come to an end. It suggests negative thoughts that threaten you.

It was fear that made the servant of Elisha cried out when he saw the Syrian army, surrounded the mountain with weapons of war (2 Kings 6:14).

Fear can make you throw away valuable things and run when nobody pursues. Do you remember when you were younger and you walk through scary places like a burial ground and your mind begins to race in fear, and your legs become shaky? Then your mind begins to imagine all sorts of things like someone chasing you from behind. Fear puts you on your heels. Fear makes you resign to fate when you are so close to a season of honour.

Fear can make you walk out of your marriage and say your spouse man can never change. That is one of the lies the devil has sown to some marriages. Fear can make you forget your child and live as if you do not have a child. Whatever makes you have such resolve in your heart seeks to make you a fearful coward who shies away from challenges. Do not give in! Face that fear today.

Fear Is Anti-Dominion

Behold, I give unto you power to tread on serpents and scorpions, and over all the power of the enemy: and nothing shall by any means hurt you.

LUKE 10:19

Although many Christians know this scripture, they still live in fear. Fear inhibits many Christians from walking in dominion.

There are too many things around that scare us from confronting everything that is robbing us of our inheritance. There are stories of how boasting Christians died mysteriously on being visited by witches. Such stories have ensnared the minds of some Christians in the bonds of fear.

Unknown to many, fear is a yoke. It controls and influences the direction a captured life goes. No one other than God should be in charge of your life. Anything else seeking to control your life aims to keep you subjective and out of the sphere of dominion.

Just to re-affirm to you: as a Christian, you are firmly plugged into the hand of God and no power of hell can open His palm and unplug you. Thus, do not be afraid to exercise your right in Christ Jesus. His death and resurrection are not tricks to daze you; they are realities. If you embrace Jesus, confidence in His name will produce more miracles through you. Beloved, I charge you to stop living in fear.

When Jesus said that He has given you power to tread on snakes and scorpion, He was not lying. He was not trying to get your hopes high and dash them when confronted with real-life situations. The power He gave you can change anything and anyone. There is no other power as great as His – none other can match His.

Do not run around seeking for power. Do not bow to the devil and dance to the church to play religion at the same time; you will not be deceiving anyone but yourself and putting yourself at a disadvantage.

Jesus has given you a power that is above every other power. Little wonder, men in the secret cult run to the church when they are tired of serving the devil and they are perpetually under threat of death.

For in it the righteousness of God is revealed from faith to faith; as it is written, "The just shall live by faith."

ROMANS 1:17

For we walk by faith, not by sight.

2 CORINTHIANS 5:7

And since we have the same spirit of faith, according to what is written, "I believed and therefore I spoke," we also believe and therefore speak,

2 CORINTHIANS 4:13

The module for living for everyone called "just" is faith. Every believer is meant to live by faith, not sight and faith is a spirit.

Faith is not exercised in silence; it becomes active by declarations. If we believe God for something, we speak it. For instance, if we believe God will heal, then we speak healing. If you believe God will deliver you, then you speak deliverance because faith is a spirit. When you speak by faith, you generate a spiritual energy that will unseat the enemy.

A child that had a hole in his heart and the parents were advised to book a flight to India where the boy will be operated on, but they had no money with them. The only option they had left was faith. Thus, the man and his wife agreed to start waking up at midnight with their baby lying in the cot. Every night they had a vigil; the spoke every scripture on healing on the boy and made declarations by faith to close the hole in the boy's heart. They did this for three weeks. While they were praying during the third week, the boy cried out. They took the boy to the hospital to check him and found out that the hole had closed completely.

Everything around you responds to words. You have to consistently speak the right words into your situation and your environment. Mountains will move when you say they should without any form of doubt in your heart. The great mountains before Zerubbabel were made plain (Zechariah 4:7). Jesus said, "If you have faith like a mustard seed, you will say to this mountain" (Matthew 17:20).

Stirring the Dominion Anointing

And, behold, I send the promise of my Father upon you: but tarry ye in the city of Jerusalem, until ye be endued with power from on high.

LUKE 24:49

There is a power that comes when a man is full of the Spirit of God. To be endued with the Spirit of God is to be clothed with the Spirit of God, which comes with power. Anyone endued with the spirit of God has the power of God and he or she becomes untouchable.

The Holy Spirit is the dispenser of the anointing. Without the Holy Spirit, the anointing that breaks yokes and wrought deliverance cannot be made available. Hence, to have the full expression of the anointing, the Holy Spirit must stir it up. The stirring of the anointing by the Holy Spirit results in victory over principalities and powers, rulers of darkness and every wicked spirit that oppresses.

Worship is the first tool for stirring the anointing. Try to observe people who expend so much anointing during their ministrations; you will discover that they are men who have cultured themselves to worship God. They do anything just to worship God: they could sing a song that has not been heard before; they dance, they clap, they could lie face down on the floor or even roll on the floor, all to worship God and stir up the anointing.

Elisha says for me to tell you what is going to happen, bring me a minstrel, a worshipper (2 Kings 3:15).

That statement underlines the importance of a worship team in a church. Churches should invest massively into their worship team. This team would make stirring of the anointing easy and convenient for the pastor. They would be able to pick sounds that have not been heard before and just follow the leadings of the Spirit to release that sound on earth.

If the only time you dance passionately is when you are in a public gathering where there is a lot of heavy beats, then you are just doing a “social function”. Practice staying in your closet to dance and worship passionately before God. The fruit of your spiritual demonstration in your closet will be evident when you get to the public place.

Worship humbles you; it is an expression of your dependence and reliance on God. The Holy Spirit is a helper, he is a lifter.

The Anointing at Work

The Spirit of the Lord is upon me, because he hath anointed me to preach the gospel to the poor; he hath sent me to heal the brokenhearted, to preach deliverance to the captives, and recovering of sight to the blind, to set at liberty them that are bruised, to preach the acceptable year of the Lord.

LUKE 4:18-19

The Anointing Breaks Yokes

When the anointing is stirred, dominion is inevitable. The anointing makes you so audacious to confront yokes.

And it shall come to pass in that day, that his burden shall be taken away from off thy shoulder, and his yoke from off thy neck, and the yoke shall be destroyed because of the anointing.

ISAIAH 10:27

Yokes place restrictions on the bearers. But when it is broken, you gain freedom and also have dominion.

The Anointing Gives Understanding

Giving alms to the poor is not a lasting solution to their predicament; it is rather a temporary solution that will make them return to ask for more. But, when you preach to the poor, you are giving them access to something that will give them dominion in life. The poor do not need sermons that will appeal to their emotion; they need the preaching of the gospel that gives knowledge and understanding that will inform them on the principles to apply to their situation to walk in true dominion.

Do not just give people money; this will only make them dependent. Educate them on potential enterprises they can venture into and how to manage it prudently. The anointing brings clear understanding to end poverty and give financial dominion (1 John 2:27).

The Anointing Heals the Brokenhearted

To heal the brokenhearted is to minister to those who have an emotional crisis. Are there people out there having an emotional crisis? Yes! Go to different homes, you will meet with women who are suffering lots of disappointments from their husband. Some men are emotionally unstable because their wife is giving them so much trouble at home. But when one is anointed, the emotional crisis can be healed

The Anointing Liberates the Captive

When the anointing comes, one can boldly proclaim liberty for everyone that is held bound in captivity. To deliver anyone in captivity is not by appealing or by making petitions, it is by bold proclamation, and that proclamation is only potent by the anointing.

There was a donkey tied to a tree, certain men were surrounding the donkey, and supervising the donkey never to gain freedom Jesus told His disciples to make a proclamation when they get to where the cot was tied (Mark 11:1-6). Even when anyone challenges them, they should proclaim their purpose there: "The master has need of it..."

The Anointing Initiates Recovery

David and his men returned home from their victory over Ziklag to discover that their wives and properties have all been carted away. With so much pain and agony, David asked God if he could pursue the captors. God permitted him to pursue and not just that, he would recover all (1 Samuel 30:1-8).

By the anointing you can recover all that the enemy has stolen from you. If you can recover all you have lost to the enemy, you will be restored to a vantage position that makes you have dominion over your enemies.

ACKNOWLEDGEMENT

My most profound gratitude goes to our Lord Jesus Christ for paying the sacrificial price to redeem and restore us to the place of Dominion.

I am deeply grateful to God for my wife, Stellamaris, who deeply understands dominion and has partnered with me in continuously exercising dominion; and our four mighty children for establishing themselves as a force to reckon with wherever they go.

I appreciate the tireless effort of Bro. Isaac Olawole and Bro. Caleb Olubere for their efforts in preparing this book for publication.

God bless you all tremendously.

ABOUT THE AUTHOR

Samson Ajetomobi

REV. SAMSON AJETOMOBI is the President of The Men of Issachar Vision Incorporated (MIV), which commenced in 1989. He is a man called by God with the mandate to reach the unreached at all cost and reawaken the Church to her responsibilities. He is gripped with a great passion for souls in reaching the unreached at all cost. Since the inception of MIV ministry, his strong drive has helped several lives to discover the essence of living for God.

He is much sought after in trainings, conferences, crusades and church revivals across the continents and because of his leadership thrust of over 34 years he is involved with the leadership of several Christian organizations and mission agencies.

He is married to Stella and their marriage is blessed with four young adults.